MORE AH MO

Indian Legends from the Northwest

Collected and told by Judge Arthur E. Griffin
Edited by Trenholme J. Griffin

hancock
house

ISBN 0-88839-303-2
Copyright © 1993 Trenholme James Griffin

Cataloging in Publication Data
Griffin, Arthur, 1862-1947.
  More Ah mo

  ISBN 0-88839-303-2

1. Indians of North America—Northwest, Pacific—Leg-
  ends. 2. Legends—Northwest, Pacific I. Griffin,
  Trenholme J. II. Title.
E78.N77G75 1992 398.2'089'970795 C92-091357-1

Production: Herb Bryce

Published simultaneously in Canada and the United States by

HANCOCK HOUSE PUBLISHERS LTD.
19313 Zero, Avenue, Surrey, B.C. V4P 1M7
(604) 538-1114   Fax (604) 538-2262

HANCOCK HOUSE PUBLISHERS
1431 Harrison Avenue, Box 959, Blaine, WA 98231-0959
(206) 354-6953   (604) 538-2262

MORE
AH MO

Your religion was written upon tables of stone by the iron finger of your God so that you could not forget. The red man could never comprehend nor remember it. Our religion is the traditions of our ancestors—the dreams of our old men, given them in solemn hours of night by the Great Spirit; and the visions of our sachems; and it is written in the hearts of our people.

Men come and go like the waves of the sea. A tear, a tamanamus, a dirge and they are gone from our longing eyes forever. It is the order of Nature. Even the white man, whose God walked and talked with him as friend to friend, is not exempt from the common destiny. We may be brothers, after all. We shall see.

Every part of this country is sacred to my people. Every hillside, every plain and grove has been hallowed by some fond memory or some sad experience of my tribe. Even the rocks, which seem to lie dumb as they swelter in the sun or darken in the rain along the silent seashore in solemn grandeur, thrill with the memories of past events connected with the lives of my people.

CHIEF SEALTH

For my children, Tessa and Tren.
To help them understand the importance
of reading and learning from the past.

Contents

Introduction

This book contains legends collected by Judge Arthur E. Griffin from Pacific Northwest Indian tribes. The legends were told to Judge Griffin by Indian storytellers between 1884 and 1947. The Judge, like other Victorians, wrote in a wordy and complex style. Judge Griffin's great-grandson has edited the stories for contemporary readers. This book is a companion to another book of legends entitled *Ah Mo: Indian Legends from the Northwest,* which was published by Hancock House in 1990.

The Pacific Northwest Indian storytellers who originally told the *Ah Mo* legends were skilled at bringing each of the characters and animals in the legend to life through gestures, varied voices, and animal calls. Since the storytellers lived with the birds, fish, and animals, few secrets were hidden from their keen vision. The legends were told in the lights and shadows around open fires, which gave the stories a magical quality. Some of the Indian storytellers were professionals who traveled from village to village. Each tribe had one or two elders who were known to be the best storytellers. The

Indian children were required to pay strict attention when a legend was being told. To prove they were listening, the children were instructed to say "Ah Mo" at frequent intervals. As the "Ah Mos" diminished, the children were whisked off to bed.

The legends in this book took place a long time ago when people, animals, mountains, rocks, trees, plants, and forces of nature (such as snow and rain) could talk to each other. Animals argued with each other, dug for roots to eat and competed in sporting contests. A sparrow could marry a hawk or a spider fall in love with a grasshopper. Bears could remove their skins like a coat and a raven borrow the eyes of a seagull.

The animals in the legends were much bigger than they are today. Some animals described in the legends were known for being quarrelsome and others for being greedy. The Indians referred to the time in which the legends took place as having been "before the change."

Some of the characters in the legends are difficult to describe because they have no equivalent in Western literature. For example, many of the Salish tribes refer to an evil old woman who had a number of mystical powers. The Indian word for this character is *Tatlashea* (she is also known as *Squiok*). The stories in *More Ah Mo* refer to her as a witch, since this is the translation Judge Griffin used to describe her. Other translators refer to this evil woman as an ogress. The best description would be somewhere

9

in between. What powers this evil witch had varied from story to story and from tribe to tribe. In a given story, Tatlashea may be able to turn a rabbit into a wolf and yet not be able to swim. Some storytellers describe Tatlashea as blind, while others note that she has very poor eyesight. The best way to deal with this translation problem is to use your imagination and not get stuck on literal descriptions. Each story should be read as separate and distinct from stories of other tribes.

Similarly, titles such as "chief" and "brave" were not used in the times before the change, but we use them here because they are current terms which we can understand. Also, the editor's great-grandfather claimed that the geographic shapes described in some of these legends were authentic.

The Northwest Indians believed that many people and animals had a guardian spirit or *tamanamus* who protected and watched over them. The guardian spirit usually took the form of an animal and had magical powers which allowed people and animals to escape danger and perform heroic deeds.

Young Indian boys and a few brave girls ventured alone into the forest, out on Puget Sound or up a mountain, hoping for a sign informing them which animal was their guardian spirit. Some lucky Indians actually spoke with their guardian spirit. Chief Sealth, the man who gave the city of Seattle its name, discovered as a young man that his guardian spirit was the seagull. The eagle, bear, wolf, elk, and raven were very desirable spirit guardians.

Pacific Northwest Indian legends, like legends from all cultures, represent more than just entertainment. They represent an attempt to explain natural phenomenon as well as teach ethical principles and pass on the history of the tribe. Psychologist-educator Bruno Bettelheim has observed that legends are unique, not only as a form of literature but as works of art which are fully comprehensible to the child, as is no other form of art. Many psychologists believe that myths are stories that come out of our collective unconscious. Author Joseph Campbell spent much of his life studying the universal nature of myths and has written extensively about his findings. The editor hopes that the *Ah Mo* stories will be enlightening as well as entertaining.

1

Tatlashea and the Children

A Chehalis Legend

A long time ago, a young girl named Chietsum lived with her family near today's Skookumchuck River. Her father, who was named Seloyum, was the oldest and wisest of the Chehalis chiefs. Chietsum lived in a longhouse made of split cedar logs with her father, mother, and two brothers. A large fire was nearly always burning in the center of the longhouse. The smoke rose from the longhouse through an opening in the roof. When the smoke was not too thick and no clouds were overhead, Chietsum could see stars through the hole in the roof before she went to sleep.

Although Chietsum was only seven years old, she was often asked to help her mother dig roots in a small meadow near her home. Chietsum loved to play with the small animals that lived in the alder trees more than she liked to dig for roots. Chietsum's mother warned her to always stay close since the evil witch Tatlashea was known to walk through the woods in search of young children.

One spring day, despite her mother's warnings, Chietsum chased Chipmunk into the woods. Chietsum ran after Chipmunk until she reached the Skookumchuck River. Chipmunk escaped from Chietsum by running into a small hole in a pine tree. When Chietsum turned around and began to walk toward the meadow, she saw a very old woman carrying a large basket on her back. The old woman's face was ugly and lined with wrinkles. Chietsum saw that she was bent nearly to the ground and was only able to stand by supporting herself with a crooked wooden walking stick.

Chietsum called a greeting to the old woman, but she did not answer. Instead, the old woman dropped her basket and walked toward Chietsum. The young child was so frightened by the ugly old woman that she couldn't move. The old woman quickly grabbed Chietsum and dropped her in the large basket. Chietsum cried out to her mother for help, but she was too far away. The old woman then securely tied the basket lid with strong rope made of woven cedar bark.

The old woman continued on her way, searching for young children. A few hours later, she was able to grab a young boy named Pauk and toss him into the basket with Chietsum. Pauk had seen the old woman before and knew that she was Tatlashea. When Pauk told Chietsum that they had been captured by the evil witch, Chietsum began to cry. Chietsum was very frightened and wondered whether she would ever see her family again.

When the sun was at its hottest, Tatlashea started to walk back toward the longhouse where she lived. The trail was bumpy and the young children were thrown back and forth as the old woman walked. While both children were very frightened, they tried to find a way to escape from Tatlashea's basket. Fortunately, Chietsum's guardian spirit, Eagle, learned that Chietsum was in danger and appeared on the lid of the basket. Eagle patiently waited for a chance to help Chietsum and Pauk.

Suddenly and without warning, the rocking of the basket stopped. The children then heard running water. The guardian spirit used this chance to push a sharp stone knife through a crack in the basket. Chietsum saw the knife and knew just what to do. She swiftly cut each of the ropes holding the basket lid in place. Chietsum and Pauk then carefully peeked out from under the lid of the basket. The children saw Eagle flying just behind them. They also saw that Tatlashea was crossing the Skookumchuck River in a large canoe. The children dropped the basket lid and patiently waited for the evil old witch to reach the other side of the river.

After crossing the river, Tatlashea continued walking toward her house. Eagle flew close to the basket and quietly told the children to watch carefully for a passing tree branch and to grab it when they had the chance. Sure enough, Tatlashea passed under a large hemlock tree and a branch came within their reach. Chietsum and Pauk grabbed the branch and held on with all of their strength. As Tatlashea walked away from the tree, the children were left hanging on the branch. Eagle then helped the children to the ground by rolling a large stone beneath them.

As soon as the children were on the ground, Eagle called Crow and told him to lead the children home. Crow complained, as was his nature, but agreed to show Chietsum and Pauk the way back to their village. Crow led the children through the forest until they came to the Skookumchuck River.

On the bank of the river, the children met a beautiful woman carving a canoe with a tool made of stone, who was actually a good fairy named Cloque.

"Please take us across the river in your canoe," pleaded Chietsum.

"We have just escaped from Tatlashea's basket," added Pauk.

Cloque quickly lifted the two children into her canoe and paddled them across the river. Cloque knew Tatlashea would discover that the children had escaped and would chase after them. When the children reached the other side of the river, they thanked the beautiful woman and continued to follow Crow toward their home. As soon as Cloque turned her canoe around and began to paddle, she saw Tatlashea standing on the opposite riverbank.

"Have you seen my children?" asked Tatlashea, pretending to be a worried mother.

"Yes," answered Cloque. "I just took them across the river."

"Take me to the other side," demanded Tatlashea rudely. "I must catch my children before they get lost."

Cloque frowned and said, "My canoe is not finished and is very unstable. It is only safe for one person to ride in this canoe."

"I will sit in the bottom and be very still," promised the evil old witch.

"We will need more weight to keep the canoe steady," said Cloque in a worried tone of voice. "You must tie a big rock on each side of your dress."

After Tatlashea had tied the rocks to her dress, she started to step toward the canoe.

"We still need more weight," said Cloque, as she handed five stones to Tatlashea and demanded that the old witch tie them in her hair.

The evil old witch did as she was told since she was anxious to get the children. Only when the stones were securely tied did Cloque let Tatlashea sit in the canoe.

"Hurry," pleaded Tatlashea as she pointed anxiously toward the opposite shore. "I may never see my children again."

"The river is very swift," answered Cloque. "You must sit very still."

Cloque carefully moved the canoe into the strong river current. Just when they were at the center of the river, Cloque began to rock the canoe back and forth. The old witch screamed for Cloque to stop, but the good fairy ignored her. Within a few seconds, the canoe turned over and dumped Tatlashea and Cloque into the icy cold river. Cloque, like all fairies, was a strong swimmer and was easily able to swim to shore. Tatlashea was not a good swimmer and, with the added weight of the stones, she quickly began to sink into the river.

Tatlashea called for help, but Cloque ignored her cries and disappeared into the woods.

Tatlashea slowly sank into the water and was never seen again. To this day, large waves can often be seen at the spot in the Skookumchuck River where the evil old witch disappeared. Tatlashea makes these waves as she tries to rise from the bottom of the river.

Eagle had watched Tatlashea drown in the river and quickly flew to tell Chietsum the good news. When Chietsum's father, Chief Seloyum, learned that the evil old witch would never again harm the children of his people, he held a great potlatch to celebrate.

2

The Pretty Young Wolf

A Puyallup Legend

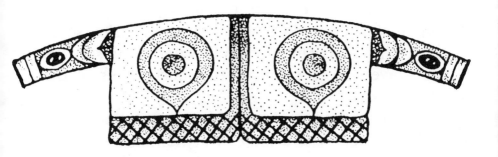

A long time ago, the Puyallup tribe was the largest and the most powerful of the Salish tribes. Most of the tribe lived under big alder trees which sheltered their canoes from the wind and rain. The people called this place "Chevalup," which means "sheltered camp." It is the place where the Puyallup River of today meets Puget Sound.

The tribe was once led by a chief who was both wise and fair. The chief had a handsome son who was great hunter and the favorite of all the tribe's maidens. This young brave had never married since he was more interested in hunting elk and catching salmon than in the attention of the maidens.

In the sixteenth summer of the young brave's life, the chief decided to test his son to determine whether he would be able to lead the tribe some day. The chief wanted to know whether his son was as brave and as smart as the most clever of the animals.

On the longest day of the summer, one of the tribe's elders saw a large wolf hunting along the banks of the river in a place where children of the tribe would often play. The chief immediately asked his son to find and kill the wolf.

The young brave was very excited by his father's request. He knew that this was a test of his skill and bravery, and he was determined not to fail. He threw his bow and a large number of his best arrows into his cedar canoe and began paddling up the river. Since the young brave had left so quickly, he didn't have time to pack any food. The brave was so anxious to find the wolf that he didn't even take time to eat any of the wild berries or roots which grew in abundance along the river.

After searching the riverbanks for five suns without any sign of the wolf, the young brave began to get very tired. As the brave had done every night before, he dragged the canoe from the river and placed it in a large vine maple tree which grew out over the river. On this night, the brave was so tired that he fell into a very deep sleep as soon as he climbed into the canoe and covered himself with his blanket.

Soon after the young brave fell asleep, a mother wolf and her pretty young daughter passed under the tree in which the young brave was sleeping. The wolves smelled the brave and decided to investigate. Encouraged by her mother, the pretty young wolf was brave enough to walk up the sloping tree trunk and peek into the canoe.

"He smells very fresh," said Pretty Young Wolf to her mother.

Pretty Young Wolf then pulled down the blanket which concealed the young brave's head. When she put her mouth close to the brave's, she felt his warm breath and realized he was alive. Since the moon was shining brightly, she could see his handsome face. Pretty Young Wolf instantly fell in love with the young brave.

"Let's eat him," suggested Mother Wolf.

"No, he's too fresh," said Pretty Young Wolf. She had decided to save his life. "We should take him home so the other wolves don't share our dinner."

"I'm so hungry," replied Mother Wolf. "Why don't we eat him now?"

"We don't have time," answered Pretty Young Wolf. "The stars are almost gone. If we stay here much longer we will be in too much danger."

The mother and daughter wolf quickly lifted the young brave out of the canoe. By using the brave's blanket as a sling, the wolves took the young man to their den and laid him on Pretty Young Wolf's bed of soft grasses. Mother Wolf was very tired and soon fell asleep. When Pretty Young Wolf was sure her mother was asleep, she hurried outside of the den and gathered some magic plants that were growing nearby. She then placed the plants under the noses of the young brave and her mother, causing both of them to sleep even more soundly.

Pretty Young Wolf then ran toward the giant mountain, which was covered with ice even in the summer. At a secret place near the base of the mountain, she hoped to find the big elk that was her spirit guardian. She found Elk just as he was about to leave the secret hiding place where he had spent the night.

"What could you want so early in the morning?" asked Elk.

"I want you to do me a great favor," answered Pretty Young Wolf.

Elk had an idea what Pretty Young Wolf wanted even before she asked. Elk had young daughters of his own and from the shy manner in which Pretty Young Wolf spoke, he suspected that she was in love.

Pretty Young Wolf told Elk all about the young brave and admitted that she was in love with him. She knew that she could not marry him as long as she was a wolf. She begged Elk to change her into a girl so she could become his wife.

"I'll grant your wish," said Elk. "But first you will need a maiden's clothing. The blind witch, who the people call Tatlashea, lives in a longhouse where the salt water [Puget Sound] narrows and runs swiftly like a river. During Tatlashea's many years of evil deeds, she has taken clothing from many maidens, including a beautiful dress that she took from the daughter of a chief.

"As soon as you are inside Tatlashea's house, find the dress which belonged to the princess and go to the nearby pond. Hang the dress on a bush so that it is reflected in the clear water. You must then dive into the water. When you return to the surface, you'll no longer be a wolf, but a girl. The clothes will fit you perfectly. But remember, all of this will happen only if you promise to be a loving wife. If you do not truly believe what you say, you will come out of the water as blind as Tatlashea."

Pretty Young Wolf thanked Elk and ran as fast as she could to Tatlashea's house. Fortunately, the old witch was not at home. Pretty Young Wolf went into the house and found a great pile of beautiful clothing. On top of the pile was a dress which was more beautiful than any clothing she had ever seen. Pretty Young Wolf quickly took the dress and hung it where Elk had told her.

Pretty Young Wolf then dove into the reflection of the dress in the cool water. The water was very deep and icy cold. When Pretty Young Wolf reached the bottom of the pond, she noticed a string of beads lying on the bottom of the pool. To her delight, she found that the beads were made from the teeth of an elk. She grasped the beads in her paw and brought them to the surface. When Pretty Young Wolf climbed out of the water and stood up, she found that she was standing on two feet rather than four.

The water in the pool soon became quiet. When Pretty Young Wolf looked into the reflection on the surface of the water, she saw a young maiden who was fabulously beautiful. Happy to learn she was no longer a wolf, she put on the lovely dress. To her surprise, it fit her perfectly. The dress was made of soft buckskin, which was deeply fringed at the bottom as well as around the sleeves and neck. Above the fringe on the skirt was a border of porcupine quills. After putting on the dress, she placed the string of elk's teeth around her neck. Thinking only of the young brave and hoping she would be worthy of him, she ran back to the den where she had left him sound asleep.

When the young brave finally awakened in the dark wolfs' den, he was frightened. He immediately ran to the mouth of the wolfs' den, where he saw many bones strewn over the ground. The young brave knew he was in danger and returned to where he'd been sleeping to see if he could find his tomahawk. As he was searching for the tomahawk, the young brave saw the loveliest maiden he had ever seen walk into the den. She was dressed in the beautiful clothing of a princess. Her long black hair was damp and hung around her shoulders in heavy strands.

The girl slowly approached the young brave and said, "Don't be afraid, this wolfs' den is my home. Come with me and I will guide you home."

"Impossible," cried the young brave. "How could I allow a beautiful princess to live in a wolf's den? If this is your home, I will remain to protect you from the wolves. But I will never be happy unless you return with me to my tribe and become my wife."

The young maiden was overjoyed and quickly accepted the young brave's marriage proposal. They were married a few days later and lived the happiest of lives together.

3

Coyote and the Salmon

A Yakima Legend

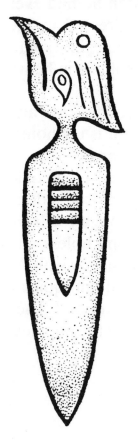

A long time ago, the animals were very hungry because there were not enough roots and berries to eat. The animals held a council meeting and decided that Coyote should travel to the ocean and bring fish up the big river that is now named the Columbia. The animals chose Coyote partly because he was a swift runner, but mostly because he was clever enough to persuade the fish to swim such a long distance. Coyote left immediately for the ocean. As Coyote traveled along the Columbia River toward the ocean, he reached a spot where a large rock blocked his path. Eagle, who was flying overhead, told Coyote that he must give Rock a present to continue his journey toward the ocean.

"Do not try to pass Rock without giving him a gift," called out Raven, confirming Eagle's advice.

Coyote had only a small blanket to give Rock. Even before Coyote had reached Rock, he was very cold, in spite of wearing his warm blanket. He shivered and shook as the cold wind blew strongly. To make things worse, Coyote saw that Rock already had many warm blankets.

"Please Rock," begged Coyote, "let me pass without giving you my only blanket."

Rock shook with anger when he heard Coyote's request.

"I am very cold and if I give you my little blanket, I will surely freeze in the cold," pleaded Coyote.

As soon as Coyote was finished speaking, Rock shook even more than before.

Coyote tried to look as humble as he could. "Let me take my poor, worn little blanket with me to keep warm and I will give it to you in the Spring when I come back along this path."

Rock shook so violently that Coyote was afraid for his life. Coyote threw his blanket and ran passed Rock as fast as he could. When Coyote stopped running, he quickly became very cold. Coyote was very sorry he had given Rock his blanket and started making a plan to get his blanket back. Coyote waited until dark and then quietly crawled back to Rock, picked up his blanket, and started to run away. After taking only a few steps, Coyote heard the noise.

"Thumpity, thump, tumble and bump, thumpity thump, tumble and bump."

Looking back over his shoulder, Coyote saw Rock rolling over and over after him. The noise made by Rock was very loud and made the whole earth tremble. Smaller rocks set loose by Rock made the noise, "Bump, bump, bumpity, jump."

Although Coyote ran as fast as he could, Rock was gaining on him. Coyote leaped aside just in time as Rock caught up with him and rolled passed, nearly crushing him.

"Run to the marsh," called a shrill voice. Coyote knew this voice was Eagle, his hunting partner, who wished to help him. Many times on cold, winter days, Eagle and Coyote had hunted together for Rabbit in the sagebrush. Eagle would fly over the sagebrush and pounce down on Rabbit when Coyote chased him out from under the branches of a protecting bush. Eagle would always share his meal with Coyote.

Coyote took Eagle's advice and ran toward the marsh. When Rock finally turned around and began to chase Coyote, it made the noise, "thumpity bump, thumpity bump." Coyote had barely run into the swamp when Rock plunged just behind him into the soft mud with a big splash. Much to his surprise and anger, Rock could not turn over.

Rock still remains half buried in the marsh, just where it rolled over for the last time. And today, when snow covers the ground and the wind blows cold, Eagle and Coyote can be seen hunting together for Rabbit. But, because Coyote owes Eagle a favor, Eagle no longer shares his meal with his hunting partner.

As soon as Coyote escaped from Rock, he ran as fast as he could toward the ocean. The journey was long, but Coyote ran day and night. When Coyote finally reached the shore of the ocean, he called to the fish from the beach. Salmon and her large family were the only fish who didn't know of Coyote's reputation for trickery and would listen.

"What do you want?" answered Salmon.

Coyote yelled as loudly as he could, "I want to take you to a safe place to raise your children."

Coyote then described the peaceful waters of the streams which flowed into the upper Columbia River.

Coyote knew that little children of Salmon were too often eaten by larger fish. He thought Salmon would surely want to go up the river to the shallows where her young children could be safe. When Salmon heard of this place, she was overjoyed and agreed to follow Coyote up the Columbia River. Coyote, Salmon, and her children left at once. Coyote ran along the riverbank and Salmon and her children followed him by swimming up the river.

As Coyote walked along the river, he eventually became very tired. He decided to rest on a sandy riverbank. Hawk saw that Coyote was sleeping and decided to steal his eyes. Hawk carefully flew down and grabbed Coyote's eyes. Coyote woke as his eyes were stolen but he couldn't see a thing. Since Hawk laughed out loud as he flew away, Coyote knew who had stolen his eyes. He screamed for Hawk to return his eyes, but received no answer.

Coyote tried his best to walk along the bank of the river, but the rocks were rough and uneven. Since Coyote could not see, he soon stumbled and fell into the Columbia River.

Coyote floated down the river with the current until he came to a place on the riverbank where wild sunflowers grew. Coyote climbed out of the water, felt his way around, and smelled the sunflowers. Reaching up, he broke off two wild sunflower blossoms and stuck them in the empty sockets where his eyes had been. Coyote hoped the flowers would return his sight. And while he could see, he could not see very well. Still, Coyote knew that the sunflower eyes were better than no eyes at all.

Hawk decided to hide Coyote's eyes on a cliff. Coyote had many enemies and when Hawk told them about stealing Coyote's eyes, many animals and birds who had been tricked by Coyote were very happy. They quickly sent Raven to the cliff to be sure that Hawk was telling the truth. The animals and birds wanted to be sure that Coyote was really blind and could no longer see them.

Coyote traveled slowly along the riverbank until he came to the home of the evil old witch, Tatlashea, who was still alive in those days. Coyote hardly recognized Tatlashea since she was wearing a mask and a fine wool blanket over her body.

"Where are your two beautiful daughters?" Coyote asked sweetly of Tatlashea, who was standing in the doorway of her house.

Tatlashea, who was blind, answered, "Coyote lost his eyes and my daughters have gone to get them for me so I can see again."

"It is terrible to be blind," agreed Coyote.

Tatlashea held out her hands to Coyote. "Being blind makes it hard to find your way. Will you please guide me to my sweathouse?"

"Certainly, if you tell me where it is," answered Coyote. Coyote managed to find the sweathouse which was located a short walk down the river. When they arrived, Tatlashea said good-bye to Coyote and thanked him for helping her. Tatlashea took off her blanket and mask and placed them on the doorstep. She then built a fire to heat the stones. When the stones were red hot, Tatlashea poured water on the stones to make hot steam for her bath.

As soon as Tatlashea closed the door to the sweathouse, Coyote put on Tatlashea's blanket and mask. Coyote fitted the eyeholes of the mask snugly around his sunflower eyes and then returned to Tatlashea's house and waited for the girls to come home. Coyote was determined to get his own eyes back again by tricking the daughters.

Finding the door unlocked, he went into the main room and lay down in front of the fire. Coyote covered his bushy tail with Tatlashea's blanket. The wind blew through the doorway and quickly covered Coyote with ashes. Since Coyote was wearing the mask and blanket and was covered with ashes, the girls thought that he was their mother.

"Have you brought me Coyote's eyes, dear daughters?" politely asked Coyote, who pretended to be just waking up and so managed to make his voice sound much like Tatlashea's.

"We had a hard time convincing Hawk to give Coyote's eyes to us," said the younger girl.

"Put Coyote's eyes in my sockets," ordered Coyote, who had hidden his sunflower eyes under the blanket when the two daughters were not looking. The girls obeyed, still believing him to be their mother. As the girls placed Coyote's eyes back in his head, they saw the thick hair on his face.

"Mother, what has made the hair on your face grow so thick and long?" asked the older girl.

"Old people are not pretty," snapped Coyote rudely.

"Can you see us now, Mother?" asked the younger daughter.

"I can see just a little, my daughters," answered Coyote. "Please get me something to eat. I am very hungry."

The girls brought food to him and placed it on some flat rocks which served as plates. When Coyote stood up to eat the food, the blanket fell off him. The daughters immediately recognized Coyote. The girls were so frightened they ran out of the house as fast as their legs could carry them.

After the girls had gone, Coyote ate all of the food he could find. He then took off Tatlashea's mask and ran from the house. Coyote was glad to have his own eyes back again, but the sunlight hurt them and he could not see well, so he found a dark cave and lived there in the dim light. After many suns, his eyes gradually became stronger. A few months later, Coyote could see as well as ever. Tatlashea remained blind the rest of her life.

The other animals were sorry that Tatlashea's daughters had been tricked by Coyote. But the children of the people who lived near the river were glad that the evil old witch did not get Coyote's eyes because Tatlashea would have been much more able to find them when they played far from home and disobeyed their mothers if she had good vision.

Coyote then continued his journey up the Columbia River with Salmon and her children. The journey was hard and in some places Salmon and her children had to jump over great waterfalls and swim up strong rapids. Coyote, Salmon, and her family eventually reached Ce-li-lo Falls.

But by then, the old witch Tatlashea was camping near these falls with her two daughters. Salmon and her children found it hard to jump over the falls, so they rested in the pool below. As the fish rested in the water, Tatlashea's daughters spotted them. The evil old witch quickly cut down some tall cottonwood trees. The trees were then made into poles that she fastened together with rope. The old witch placed the heavy ends of the poles on the rocks and pointed the lighter ends out just below the falls, above the spot where the salmon were thickest. Tatlashea then placed large logs across the ends of these poles. She piled many rocks on the logs so they would not tip up with her weight when she walked out over the water to fish. Tatlashea used twine and sticks to make a round net, which she dipped into the water. When a salmon touched the cross-strings, she raised the net and grabbed the fish.

Coyote was growing very thin and hungry from his long journey up the Columbia River. When he saw the old witch, he rubbed his stomach and said, "Tatlashea, give me something to eat. I have been walking for days and I am starving."

Tatlashea pretended not to hear Coyote because of the roaring of the falls.

"Tatlashea, please give me a salmon to eat," called Coyote again.

Tatlashea ignored Coyote and kept on fishing.

"Just give me a small salmon," pleaded Coyote for the third time.

Tatlashea again pretended not to hear him. Coyote then started to walk out on the poles to where Tatlashea stood.

"Go back Coyote," pleaded Tatlashea. "You will break the poles. I can hardly catch enough salmon for myself."

Coyote knew that Tatlashea could catch all the salmon she needed. "May I sit down on your poles and rest? I am so tired."

"You may sit down on the pile of rocks, but not out here," replied Tatlashea.

By this time Coyote was very angry with Tatlashea for being so selfish. Coyote sat down on the pile of rocks. Since Tatlashea was so busy catching salmon, she didn't notice that Coyote was carefully rolling off one big stone after another, until they were nearly all gone. Coyote then quickly jumped to the ground. This caused Tatlashea, her net, and her basketfull of Salmon's children to fall into the swift water with a great splash.

Tatlashea screamed to Coyote, "Help me, help me."

"The falls are making so much noise I can't hear you," answered Coyote.

"Oh swim out and save me," begged the evil old witch as she thrashed in the water with her thin, bony arms.

"I am too weak to swim," yelled Coyote. "If you had fed me, I would be strong enough to help you. You gave me no salmon and I am so weak."

"Then just hold out a stick to me," screamed the evil old witch.

"If you had given me just the one little salmon I would have strength to hand you a stick and help you to shore, but now I am too weak," repeated Coyote.

Tatlashea realized it was no use trying any longer to get Coyote to help her. Although Tatlashea splashed and splashed and tried to swim, the swift current quickly pulled her under the icy cold water of the Columbia River.

After the death of Tatlashea, Coyote continued to lead Salmon and her children up the Columbia River until they reached the animal people. To this day, Salmon's children are safer from large fish than they would have been in the ocean; but the older salmon are often caught by hungry people and animals like Bear as they swim up the river to have their own children.

4

Rabbit and Grizzly Bear

A Snoqualmie Legend

A long time ago, Grizzly Bear and Rabbit found themselves traveling together along the river now called the Yakima. They were going toward the Cascade Mountains. The weather was turning cold and the sky was full of clouds.

Grizzly Bear wanted snow to fall from the clouds since the snow was his spirit guardian. Rabbit wanted the clouds to disappear since it would then get very cold. If the temperature dropped very low, the water in the river would freeze and allow Rabbit to travel swiftly on the ice.

Rabbit's song was, "Soc soc hamalie, Soc soc hamalie," which means "clear weather, clear weather."

Grizzly Bear growled, "hallis, hallis," which means "snow, snow." The weather soon turned clear and very cold. This allowed Rabbit to travel swiftly on the smooth ice. Grizzly Bear had to walk on the rough ground and make his way up the river the best he could through the thick brush. Grizzly Bear could not walk with Rabbit since the ice was not strong enough for his great weight.

Rabbit would often tease Grizzly Bear by calling to him, "What a slow walker you are. Why don't you catch up to me?"

This teasing made Grizzly Bear decide to eat Rabbit the first time he caught up with him.

"Wait for me," said Grizzly Bear. "Don't walk so fast Rabbit."

Rabbit waited until Grizzly Bear came close, then crossed to the other side of the Yakima River so Grizzly Bear couldn't catch him. As the two moved up the river, the ice kept getting thicker, so Grizzly Bear could cross the river in some places. This made things more dangerous for Rabbit.

Grizzly Bear smiled. "In the morning when Rabbit is sleeping, I will cross the river and eat him for breakfast."

When night came, Grizzly Bear pretended to sleep, but had one eye slightly open. He saw Rabbit roll himself up in his blanket and lie down to sleep by a small fire. When morning was approaching, Grizzly Bear quietly rose to his feet. As soon as Grizzly Bear saw Rabbit's fire go out, he started to walk toward him.

Rabbit had lived among coyotes for so long that he slept with both eyes open and his long ears set to catch every sound. Rabbit saw Grizzly Bear walk onto the frozen river and heard the ice cracking as Grizzly Bear moved over the ice. Rabbit quickly placed a rock under his blanket and ran behind a bush to watch Grizzly Bear try to grab him. Rabbit had long ears, but Grizzly Bear had a good nose, and it did not take Grizzly Bear long to know Rabbit was not under his blanket.

"Why are you getting up so early?" growled Grizzly Bear.

"To get an early start so as to get to Lake Keechelus before dark," answered Rabbit.

Grizzly Bear ate no breakfast, while Rabbit ate some bark he nibbled from a small tree.

That night, Rabbit arrived at Lake Keechelus and made his camp way out on the thin ice. Grizzly Bear reached the lake way after dark, and the great bear was very tired, cross, and hungry. He wanted to get a last meal before he went to sleep until spring. Rabbit called to Grizzly Bear to camp by him.

Grizzly Bear roared angrily, "If I move out on the ice, you will run away."

"No, I won't," promised Rabbit.

The big bear began to walk toward Rabbit. Grizzly Bear was now so hungry that he did not notice the ice cracking beneath him. Rabbit looked so plump and fat that Grizzly Bear licked his chops.

"How do you keep so fat?" asked Grizzly Bear.

"By walking out here where the ice is smooth," answered Rabbit.

Grizzly Bear was now very close to Rabbit. When he was only steps away, he jumped toward his dinner. Rabbit jumped at just the same time and escaped easily. Grizzly Bear landed with a great crash where Rabbit had been standing. Grizzly Bear immediately tumbled into the freezing lake water as the ice broke under him.

"Get a stick and pull me out," pleaded Grizzly Bear.

"All right," answered Rabbit, who ran to the shore and grabbed a long stick. But instead of helping Grizzly Bear, Rabbit used the stick to shove the cold and helpless Grizzly Bear under the ice.

To this day, if you go to Lake Keechelus, you may be able to see Grizzly Bear where he froze under the ice. You will also always see Rabbit sleeping with both eyes open and ears up, listening for Grizzly Bear.

5

Tatlashea and Chipmunk

A Toppenish Legend

A long time ago, Chipmunk lived with his grandmother in a large fir tree. The tree was near a creek, which people today have named Status Creek. Every summer and fall Chipmunk kept very busy helping his grandmother gather and store food for the long and cold winter. Grandmother often told Chipmunk to watch out for Tatlashea, the evil old witch.

Tatlashea had long fingernails which were as sharp as Eagle's claws. The witch used the claws to grab little children or small animals that came within her reach.

The children, who liked to play with Chipmunk, also warned him to watch out for Tatlashea. Chipmunk ignored these warnings, since he believed he could climb up trees so quickly that Tatlashea would not be able to catch him.

One day Chipmunk went far into the forest without his grandmother in search of pine nuts. Chipmunk found a large pine tree and scampered up the trunk to look for food and to see how far he had gone from home. The first time Chipmunk saw Tatlashea was when he decided to go home and looked down the tree trunk.

"Come down, my little friend," called Tatlashea sweetly.

Chipmunk was very frightened and began to chatter his teeth. "All right," answered Chipmunk. "But I must get a little more food before I come down." Chipmunk then filled his arms full of pine

43

cones and said, "Look out! I am dropping from this tree branch with the pine cones."

The pine cones dropped quickly toward the ground and Tatlashea greedily grabbed at them. Fortunately, Chipmunk had tricked the evil old witch and stayed on the limb. While Chipmunk was safe, for the moment, he was afraid to stay in the tree all night because he might fall asleep and tumble out of the tree. Worse, Owl might try to eat him.

Tatlashea waited patiently. She believed she would soon have Chipmunk for dinner. While the evil old witch was waiting for Chipmunk to come down from the tree, Chipmunk was busy thinking of a plan to escape Tatlashea. He thought and thought of a way to escape Tatlashea, until it seemed his little head would burst from thinking so hard.

Tatlashea had a plan of her own for catching Chipmunk, and pretended to fall asleep, hoping he would come down from the tree. But Chipmunk knew she was awake and trying to fool him. As the sun started to fall in the sky, Chipmunk finally thought of a plan to fool Tatlashea.

Chipmunk broke off a great number of pine branches and made them into a big ball. Chipmunk then crawled carefully into the middle of the ball and rolled forward. The ball fell off the branch and dropped right on Tatlashea's head. Tatlashea screamed, grabbed the ball of pine branches, and tore it apart, trying to find Chipmunk. Chipmunk jumped out of the pile and ran as fast as he could toward his home. Tatlashea heard Chipmunk escape and reached for him with one hand just as he was running away. Chipmunk moved so quickly that he was barely able to escape from Tatlashea's hands. But as Chipmunk ran, Tatlashea's long claws scratched the full length of his back. That was how close Chipmunk came to being caught by the evil old witch.

Many years later, when Chipmunk had grown very old, the Great Spirit turned him into a big stone that you can see when you walk along Status Creek near Mount Adams. By taking this walk, you can see for yourself the scratches on Chipmunk's back made by Tatlashea's fingernails when she grabbed to catch him.

6
The Klickitat Strongman

A Klickitat Legend

A long time ago, the Muckleshoot tribe traveled every summer to the mountain now called Huckleberry Mountain to pick berries and to snare goats that walked on trails along the mountain's rocky ridges. The Klickitat tribe also traveled in the summer to Huckleberry Mountain, to hunt deer and elk and to catch trout in the mountain streams. The two tribes camped very near one another on the mountain.

One year, the two tribes disagreed about who should get the best campsite. The chiefs of the tribes decided to hold a contest between the strongest man from each tribe to determine which tribe would get the campsite. The contest took place between the White River and the Green River at a spot a short distance above Mox-la-push where the two rivers joined. Many people from other tribes came to the contest by following the trail which ran west passed the mountain that is today called Mount Enumclaw.

As soon as the contest began, the Muckleshoot strongman pulled up several vine maple and alder trees by the roots to show how strong he was. This was impressive to everyone. But the Klickitat strongman pulled up two huge fir trees and knocked the earth and stones out of their roots by striking them against the heel of his moccasin. He then placed one of the fir trees in his right hand and used the tree to knock down all the other trees that were growing nearby. He then used the same fir tree to level all of the hills from the mountains near Cla-hol-sas (Enumclaw) to White Lake, and to where Auburn is located today. Great banks of gravel at the west side of the prairie created by the strongman still mark the place where the leveling stopped.

The Klickitat strongman was declared the winner of the contest by the chiefs.

Despite the fact that the prairie was made by a Klickitat strongman, the Muckleshoot people decided to live on this flat stretch of land. Eventually the prairie was covered with oak trees, grass, and many flowers. Numerous marshes were formed along the foothills, thanks to the industrious little beavers, who worked so hard making dams on the creeks and streams.

7

Tum Tum

A Duwamish Legend

A long time ago, an old man named Tum Tum lived in a longhouse on the Duwamish River, as it is called today. Tum Tum had fished the waters now known as Puget Sound for over sixty years. Tum Tum was now so old that he could barely see. Because of his poor eyesight, when Tum Tum finished fishing, he often would have trouble deciding which direction to paddle his canoe to reach his home. People from his tribe would have to paddle out and tow Tum Tum and his cedar canoe back home.

Because he was very old and experienced, Tum Tum knew all of the best fishing places and the easiest way to catch fish.

He knew that smelt swam close to the surface whenever dogfish were feeding on them. To catch the smelt, Tum Tum used a long, thin piece of wood with sharp spikes made from bones set close together like the teeth of a comb. Tum Tum used this wooden board like a paddle. As the canoe moved along, the smelt were speared by the sharp prongs. Every so often he would strike the board against the top of his canoe and so the little fish would fall into the boat.

When Tum Tum fished for herring, he used fish eyes and clams for bait. When Tum Tum trolled for salmon, he used two long fishing lines and a clamshell spinner. A piece of halibut, fastened on hooks made from a yew tree limb with a bone for a barb, served as bait.

When Tum Tum was fishing, he would paddle toward the shore calling "Tum Tum." If he was lucky, someone from the village would answer him, so he would know which way to go to reach his home. Tum Tum would frequently take a little boy or girl with him to guide him on his way home. When he reached the shore, Tum Tum would divide the fish he had caught with the little boy or girl.

When Tum Tum was fishing alone and the sun was shining or the day was clear, he would often paddle his canoe to the west side of Puget Sound and follow the shore until he reached an object he recognized. Tum Tum would then go ashore and cook some fish to eat.

When evening came, he would roll up in his blanket and sleep through the night. If it was raining, he would sleep under his canoe or under a large tree that gave shelter without dripping the rain.

Tum Tum cooked his fish over an open fire. He put fish on the end of a sharp stick, which he fastened in the ground in a slanting position. The stick was placed close enough to the fire so the fish would cook evenly, but not near enough to burn. To make a fire, Tum Tum used a bow-drill and a stick. The stick was usually a dry cottonwood root about a foot long. He would lay a piece of driftwood on the ground and place the stick on it in an upright position. A plentiful supply of cedar bark tinder was placed around its base. By winding a bow-string around the stick and by rapidly pushing the bow backward and forward, the stick was made to spin so quickly that the friction made heat which started a fire.

One bleak winter's day, Tum Tum was fishing for cod in deep water not far from Blake Island. The weather was so cold that none of his tribesmen would go fishing with him. Later in the afternoon, the wind came up and blew hard from the south. A few of his people on Alki Point saw Tum Tum pull up his anchor and start paddling for the eastern shore. The wind increased and the rain came in torrents, blotting everything from view. Later, when the rain stopped, neither Tum Tum nor his canoe could be seen. The people listened anxiously for Tum Tum's call. They began to fear for their friend when they heard nothing but the roaring of the wind and the crashing of the waves on the shore. The next morning, Tum Tum's friends decided to search for him. They searched for hours, but found no trace of Tum Tum.

Tum Tum's friends decided to paddle toward Blake Island, where his canoe had last been seen. The wind was blowing so hard that the water was white with spray. One man in the bow of a large canoe thought he saw a dark object ahead. After he pointed at the object, the other men began to paddle in that direction. Suddenly, the object disappeared beneath the waves. But it came into sight again shortly afterward. The object looked like an overturned black canoe with a paddle in the air.

While Tum Tum's friends paddled with all their might in an effort to overtake the canoe, the object always kept slightly ahead of them. Then, without warning, the object sank beneath the waves. One of the men later said he'd heard a voice calling, "Tum Tum, Tum Tum," when the object sank. The people knew then that Tum Tum's canoe had capsized in the storm. One of the tribe's elders told them later that Tum Tum had turned into a sea creature and that they would never see their old friend again.

The people believe that if you go out on Puget Sound when a strong wind is blowing and the waves are high, you will often see a black sea creature with a large fin raised out of the water. They believe that what you see is Tum Tum trying to right his overturned canoe.

8

Raven and Bear

A Puyallup Legend

Raven had a son and Bear had a daughter. The son and daughter were eventually married and lived in the home of Bear. One day Raven decided to visit his daughter but he found that Bear had no food to offer him. To feed his guest, Bear built a great fire and placed empty clam shells on the ground. Bear washed his paws and stood very close to the fire. He put his hands so close to the fire that the fat he was storing for the winter began to drip into the clam shells. In this way, Bear was able to feed his guest Raven.

Raven was so pleased with Bear's generosity that he invited Bear for a visit. When Bear arrived on his visit, Raven built an even bigger fire than Bear had built. Raven washed his hands and then held them close to the fire. Since Bear was so big and needed a huge meal, Raven had to hold his hands close to the fire until there was no fat left. The Bear had his meal, but all that was left of Raven's hands were skin and bones. This is why, today, Raven's hands are thin claws covered with scales.

9

The Woman Who Told Lies

A Puyallup Legend

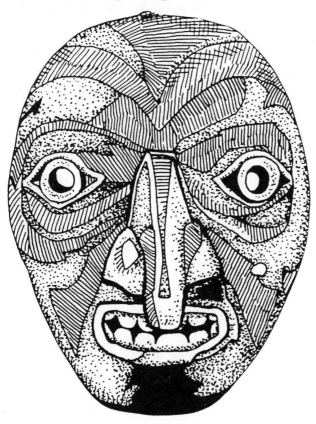

An Indian Chief was walking along the beach north of the Puyallup River when he met an old woman. The woman began telling the chief stories. Each story was more fantastic than the one before. After a time, the chief realized that the stories were lies. He grabbed the old woman's jaw and yelled, "You are a liar. I will hold your mouth open forever." The chief held her mouth open for so long that she turned to stone. You can still see her open mouth at the place the white people call Brown's Point. If you take a branch and rattle it in the mouth of the old woman, it will soon rain.

Appendix

The Language of Northwest Indians

The legends contained in this book and *Ah Mo: Indian Legends from the Northwest* were told to Judge Arthur E. Griffin in a mixture of English and Chinook. Edmond S. Meany wrote the following about the Chinook language in a booklet published in 1908:

> The popular conception that the "Chinook Language" is the "Siwash Language" is doubly incorrect. Chinook is not a language, and Siwash is not the name of the western Indian. Chinook is merely a jargon and Siwash is simply a Chinook word meaning man, and could as properly be applied to a white man if the real meaning be followed. The Chinook jargon was invented by Captain Cook and his party of explorers for use in dealing with the various tribes of Puget Sound Indians, supplemented later by Vancouver and his men, and spread broadcast by fur dealers and others. It is composed of words taken from different tribal languages, mixed with French and English words, and

is so simple in its construction that it not only served its purpose with the white man to talk with the Indian, but was speedily acquired by the different tribes themselves for use in communicating with their neighbors, for the native language of one tribe was strange to and not comprehended by another: there were thirty-six dialects on Puget Sound, all different.

Owing to its convenience this jargon spread until it was used by the Indians, and their pale-faced visitors, from the Rocky Mountains to the Pacific Ocean, and from California to Mount St. Elias in Alaska. Beyond Mount St. Elias the line was sharply drawn and the Chinook was unknown, the Indians there using their own language, with a little English and a great deal of Russian.

How the Stories Were Collected

Judge Griffin was a tireless defender of Indian rights. The headline of *The Seattle Star,* which was then the largest circulation newspaper in Washington State, screamed in huge red letters on February 23, 1927:

Indians Here Sue For $73,000,000
U.S. Failed To Keep Treaty, They Claim

Indians Say Uncle Sam Failed to Keep Promises
Made by Governor Stevens

With the arrival Wednesday of G. T. Stormont, United States attorney, Arthur E. Griffin, attorney for 13 Indian tribes in the state of Washington, started taking testimony from the various Indian tribes and old settlers in a $73,000,0000 suit he has filed in the United States court of claims. The Indians' claim goes back to the signing of the original treaties between Governor Stephens and the Indian chiefs. They claim that the government has failed to live up to these treaties and now demand the funds they say are in arrears. The case has been in course of preparation for 10 years, Griffin says.

Griffin, accompanied by Stromont, left Wednesday for the Muckleshoot Indian Reservation to take testimony from chiefs of the various tribes in the suit. Many of Washington's oldest white settlers will be called upon, Griffin said, to add their stories to those of the redskin chiefs. The two attorneys will visit each of the 13 tribes listed among the claimants.

The Duwamish, Lummi, Whidbey Island, Skagit, Upper Skagit, Swinomish, Kikiallus, Snohomish, Snoqualmie, Stillaguamish, Suquamish, Samish, Puyallup, Squaxin, Skokomish, Upper Chehalis, Muckleshoot, Nooksack, Chinook and the San Juan Island tribes of Indians are among the claimants. The agreements made in 1885, the Indians say, stipulated that the government should pay the tribe in money, and that it should erect various educational and agricultural schools in this territory. Neither of these things have been done, the Indians claim.

Indian Longhouses

To establish the Indian land claims in court, Judge Griffin collected testimony and materials on Indian longhouses, hunting grounds, and life before the white settlers arrived. The following is a description of houses built and used by the lower Skagit tribe, as written by an unknown author:

The lumber used was cedar throughout the whole longhouse. The Indian carpenters measured lumber by fathom, the length of your arms outstretched, which would be about six feet on the average. The houses were divided into compartments, which are called "wha-cha-hoose" in the Indian language. Each one of these compartments is exactly the same length (which is sixty feet or ten fathoms). All longhouses were sixty feet wide. It was the custom that each compartment be sixty feet square. Therefore, it is only necessary that you find the number of compartments in a building to determine the dimensions of it.

The shape of the building was most generally the same as a chicken house. This is a building with the roof slanted to one side giving rain water a chance to run off of the roof. It is perfectly natural then that one side of the longhouse be higher than the other. It was an advantage to the Indian carpenter that the ground upon which the building was to be built is higher on one side or has a natural slope. This enabled the carpenter to establish the slope on the roof automatically. In some houses however the roof was brought to a peak in the middle, something more or less like the modern house is made. The lumber used for the roof was hued in a "U" shape, forming a trough by itself to make a better water carrier. This shape was acquired through the aid of the shape of the tree from which the lumber is taken.

The first part to go up in the construction of a longhouse are the posts. A line of posts is set up along the side of the building to be built. The posts are placed directly across one another. Timbers hued down to the desired size were laid across, upon these posts that stand upright. The buildings were sixty feet wide, the timbers were then sixty feet long.

To get the slope necessary to run the water off of the roof, the posts on one side had to be higher or longer than on the other side. Upon these posts running across the building and resting on the post, were laid smaller timbers lengthwise of the longhouse. These smaller timbers were called "sis-la-oose." The smaller timbers are of course placed lengthwise (of the building) resting upon the larger timbers (which is crosswise of building) and resting upon the upright posts. Upon the smaller timbers, which is lengthwise of the longhouse and is uppermost, is laid the roof lumber. The lumber used for the roof would then be crosswise of the building, making use of the shape it was given when split from the tree ("U"). The first layer of the roof lumber is laid with its ends at the edge of the roof, which point the water is to run off. The next layer, toward the higher side of roof is laid with its ends where they join, lapping over the ends of the lower layer. This is followed with the next layers, and gives the rain water to run off from one layer to the next and so on to the last layer where the water runs off to the ground. The timbers which run across the (the timbers referred to here are the ones which rest upon the posts) are raised by means of a prong. Indians from all portions of the Skagit tribe gather to help raise these timbers since they are very heavy.

All around the longhouse is a slight extension about eight feet wide. The interior of the building is decorated with a very high grade of Indian wallpaper, which was made of a very rare weed that was woven into whatever design or color was desired. The posts were carved by experts who are paid very highly for this work. Designs and architecture are carved on these posts which the Indians worshipped.

The dimensions of the house varied accordingly to the number of compartments in the house. The standard measurement of each building was sixty feet square and eighteen feet high at the higher side of the roof, and fifteen feet high at the lower side of the roof. The dimensions of each house could then be found by learning the number of compartments.

Foods eaten by Skagit Indians and their English names

VEGETABLES
Indian Term and English Term

1. Sqwee-wh — Fern roots
2. Za-bby — Variety of bulb
3. Bo-bo-loh — Variety of bulb
4. Sk-wa-lh-ol — Variety of bulb
5. Ta-lach — Medical foods
6. Sha-gwack — Mild carrots
7. Chia-do — Practically the same as the modern onions
8. Bik-o-ya — Kush weeds
9. Tea-wa — Marsh ferns
10. Yo-la — Green foods raised on the flats
11. Sho-hatch — Mild roots
12. Uhcw-sha — Roots
13. Cha-laiq — Bulbs
14. Kwa-wh-oh-ks — Wild onions

BERRIES

1. Zit-gwad — Salmonberries
2. Zab-bit — Elderberries
3. She-yo — Strawberries
4. Yaiy-kub — Blueberries
5. Wa-kwull — Huckleberries
6. Ste-koug-gwad — Blackberries
7. Kwa-las-tum — Chokeberries
8. Chil-kuba — Black caps
9. Ste-ta-wh — Red huckleberries
10. Sba-b-ch — June plum
11. Shbul-kolts — Cranberries
12. Sh-ak — Thimbleberries
13. Tub-wh — Wild gooseberries
14. Chowh — Crabapples
15. Ha-had — Similar to a chokeberry
16. Ha-koawh — Hazelnuts
17. Ha-ad-light-ed — Mild currants
18. Skai-wa — Indian tobacco
19. Cle-batz — Red currants